A GIFT FOR

_____

FROM

_____

Dr. Henry Cloud
& Dr. John Townsend

What to Do When You Don't Know What to Do

Divorce & Lost Love

God Will Make a Way

INTEGRITY
PUBLISHERS

Contents

Prologue

I know it doesn't feel like it right now, but there is life after divorce." I (John) was having lunch with Michele, a friend of mine who I had known for a long time. She was an attractive, smart woman in her mid-thirties. And she had recently been divorced by her husband, Sean. The breakup had been pretty messy, and she'd been devastated by it all. That's why she had asked me to lunch, to begin to pick up the pieces of her life.

"No, it doesn't feel like it. I don't know where to start," Michele said. "I mean, I'm having to deal with being really, really hurt, plus figuring out what the single life is about, plus dealing with the kids—and all at one time. It is just over-whelming. How do I handle all this?"

I totally agreed with her. Divorce is one of the most painful experiences a person can undergo. It literally tears your life in two, at many levels. You began as a couple with intimacy, passion, desire, and all your dreams. And for whatever reason, the person you were invested in most deeply doesn't want you anymore. It is a brutal thing.

I told my friend, "Well, you are right. Honestly, it is going to be tough for a while, and there is no way around it. But I can tell you the one thing I would do that would go a long way toward helping you get through all this."

"What is it?"

"I would first plug in, get connected to some really good people."

Michele said, "So I'm ready to start dating already?"

"No, no, no," I said. "That's not the picture at all. I don't think that's your first goal. For one thing, you need some time to resolve your hurt and grief. Secondly, you need to learn whatever lessons there are in this divorce to help you prepare for falling in love again. Dating relationships aren't the primary source of support and care anyway."

"But what if I meet a guy who really cares about me?" she asked. "That would help me get the support I need to get through this."

"It could certainly be supportive; I agree with that part," I said. "But the nature of dating is that it is a tryout, an experiment, and there is no commitment until things get serious. Dating is a great thing, but I'd suggest something else for you right now."

"What?"

"I think you need a few safe, connected, caring people who aren't dating prospects—who can really be there for you on some regular basis, and who will walk you through this."

"Like counseling?" Michele asked.

"Maybe, but that's not what I was picturing," I replied. "More like getting a few friends together, or getting into a small group at church, and addressing all your struggle and hurt, and receiving their support and having them pray for you."

"What will that do? I'm still not married or dating," she said.

"Look at it this way. If you were a college football player and you broke your leg, you wouldn't spend a lot of time interviewing agents and professional team representatives. You aren't ready for them, and those people have a different agenda for you. Instead, you'd be with doctors, physical therapists, and trainers. These folks would be there for the specific purpose of getting you restored and back in shape so that you could move on. That's what a small group of supportive people would do for you. They'd get together with you to help you connect, let go and forgive, learn the lessons, and be strengthened for dealing with life again. Let's find you a group."

Michele got it, and she became involved in a small group that helped her with her pain, worked her through her divorce, and gave her the strength and power to move on. Over time, she was transformed from a devastated and hopeless person to a stable, caring, and wiser woman. As an aside, a couple of years ago—after beginning to date again once she was ready—Michele met Troy, who was perfect for her, and they are now married.

But the important point here is that while she is very happy now, Michele would never say that remarriage was how God made a way for her. Marrying Troy was the result of what God really did. The real miracle is all the grace and healing she found with a small band of women who loved her, walked with her, and helped her heal.

The main obstacle to following God's way through any crisis is failing to trust him. Most of us have little difficulty believing in God. But for some reason we balk when it comes to really trusting God. Trusting seems so simple—all we do is let go of our own solutions and place our-selves in God's hands. Yet our fallen human nature prods us to hang on to our own ways. Our doubts rage like a rising river: *Will he come through for me? Can I depend on him?*

Trust is the bridge over that river. The way God makes for you means nothing until you step on the bridge and start walking. Trust is both an attitude and an action. The more you act on your faith in God, the more you will see of his way for you. When we trust God's way, he can change even the most hopeless situation.

God is active on your behalf, even when you cannot see it. Faith calls you to be active also. This may seem like a paradox. "Am I doing it? Or is God doing it?" The answer to both questions is yes. God will do what only he can do, and your job is to do what you can do.

The God who made a way for Michele is available to you now. As the psalmist said, "The LORD is near to all who call on him, to all who call on him in truth. He fulfills the desires of those who fear him; he hears their cry and saves them" (Psalm 145:18–19).

We don't believe you are reading this book by coincidence. Even though at first Michele had no idea what she should do to overcome the devastating effects of her divorce, God had a way, and her faith healed her as she followed his directions. You will have the same experience when you exercise your faith in God by heeding the eight principles we will show you in the next section. To keep this book simple and brief, we will deal exclusively with divorce in the upcoming pages. However, the ideas presented here also apply to lost love, such as the breakup of a significant dating relationship. Though there are real differences between the two, the similarities are close enough for our goals here.

By following God's instructions, you can recover from your divorce or the loss of a significant love. Join us as we show you how to follow God's way in your life. Please read on.

PART I:
EIGHT PRINCIPLES TO GUIDE YOUR
RECOVERY FROM DIVORCE

Many people who experience divorce cannot see their future clearly. They have encountered a huge loss that they never expected would happen to them. They may feel that in some way divorce leaves a stain on their lives that will be with them for the rest of their lives. The experience is so deep and overwhelming that it leaves them feeling hopeless. They don't know what to do. They cannot see a future of happiness and recovery because they don't think it exists. But God always has a way. He doesn't intend for his people to live in misery, and those who experience divorce are every bit as much his people as anyone else.

You can find God's way through the aftermath of divorce when you activate your faith in him by following the eight principles in this section. We will have more to say specifically about the practical aspects of working through your divorce recovery in the section that follows this one. Think of these principles as foundation stones. You must lay them in your life so that you can build on them the structures you need to win over your problem.

Begin Your Journey with God

When we speak of God, we don't mean some kind of vague, universal force; we mean a real person, complete with mind, will, and the power to act in our lives. So when we say that faith and trust will carry you to recovery from your divorce, we're not talking about warm religious feelings or an exercise in positive thinking. Meaningful faith must be placed in a real Person, who knows the way for you, even when you don't, and promises to lead you on it. That's God. So our first principle for healing from your divorce losses is to *begin your journey with God.* You can't do it without him.

Your need for God's help is no more a weakness than your need for air. We did not create ourselves, nor were we designed to create our own way in life. God wired us to depend on him. When you exercise faith in him, you position yourself to accomplish superhuman feats, which is what recovering from divorce may require. You are reaching beyond human strength and knowledge and tapping into God's infinite strength and knowledge.

Most of us, when facing a difficult or painful situation that we don't know how to handle, do one of two things. First, we repeat what didn't work before, but this time we try harder. Chronic dieters, for example, try to muster up just a little more will power, and "this time it will work." Second, we stop trying altogether. *I will never stop overeating, so what's the use?* The first reaction often spawns the second. Trying to get through life on your own limited strength and knowledge leads to futility and loss of hope.

But in God's economy, getting to the end of yourself is the beginning of hope. Jesus said, "God blesses those who realize their need for him" (Matthew 5:3 NLT). When you admit that you don't know how to handle your problem and ask God for help, you transcend your own limitations and God's resources become available to you.

God's resources cannot be earned; they can only be received as a gift when we, in humility, acknowledge our need for our Creator. He is ready to get involved in your life. All you have to do is say yes to him. Then he will provide what you need to overcome the effects of even the most debilitating divorce.

Sometimes his way will be truly miraculous, and sometimes it will involve a lot of work and change on your part. Often it won't be the way you thought you needed. But when you don't know what to do and turn to God to make a way, it works.

People who

rise to the top seldom

get there alone.

They seek help.

Choose Your Traveling Companions Wisely

When I (Henry) was a youngster, Jack Nicklaus was king of golf, and as an aspiring golfer, I thought he was almost a god. Then I heard that he consulted a golf pro for help on his swing. I was stunned. Teachers were for people who didn't know what they were doing. I have learned a lot since then. People who rise to the top seldom get there alone. They seek help.

This story illustrates our second principle of God's way of recovering from divorce. *Surround yourself with people who are committed to support you, encourage you, assist you, and pray for you.*

One of the ways God works is through other people. Solomon said, "Two are better than one. . . . If one falls down, his friend can help him up. But pity the man who falls and has no one to help him up!" (Ecclesiastes 4:9–10). Some of these people will just show up in your life, sent at just the right time. Others you have to seek out. They can range from professionals to a neighbor or friend at church. Here are some important qualities to look for as you select your support team.

SUPPORT. In recovering from divorce, you are pushing uphill. The loss you have experienced can drain you of emotional, physical, and spiritual strength. You need the kind of person who will show up at your door anytime to help you.

LOVE. You need the safety net of people who love you deeply just as you are, even when you don't feel lovable.

COURAGE. You will encounter risk and fear. When the task looks too daunting to face, your support team will build your courage.

FEEDBACK. You can't see yourself objectively. You need honest people who are not afraid to correct you when you are wrong.

WISDOM. You don't have all the wisdom and knowledge you need to make it. Look for wise people through whom God will speak to you.

EXPERIENCE. Seek out the experience of others who have been through divorce and know what you are going through. They will know what to do when you don't.

MODELING. It is difficult to do what we have never seen done. Seek out and learn from those who have recovered from divorce.

VALUES. Your value system will guide you as you turn your life around. We learn values from others, and others support us by enforcing values.

Stay close to people who share your values; stay away from those who don't.

ACCOUNTABILITY. You need people who will monitor your progress and keep you on track. Look for people who will ask the tough questions: Where are you failing? What kind of help do you need?

You may already have in your life people who meet your need for support. If so, explain that you need them on your journey to recovery. Ask if they will be available to provide accountability, feedback, or support. They will probably feel honored and valued that you would ask.

If you run short of supportive friends, consider joining a structured support system, such as a Bible study group. Share with these people your struggle and ask for their prayers and input. You will be amazed how a loving support group will help you on your journey.

Place High Value on Wisdom

Often we feel hopeless and lost in our search for answers because we lack vital information about how divorce affects us. A key way out of despair is to find these missing pieces of wisdom and apply them to our problem. God tells us that wisdom produces hope: "Know also that wisdom is sweet to your soul; if you find it, there is a future hope for you, and your hope will not be cut off" (Proverbs 24:14).

So our third principle for finding God's way to recover from divorce is this: *Recognize the value and need for the missing pieces of wisdom in your life; then ask God to show them to you.*

WISDOM COMES FROM GOD. James tells us to ask God for the wisdom we need: "If any of you lacks wisdom, he should ask God, who gives generously to all without finding fault . . ." (James 1:5). God knows what to do even when you don't. Ask him for answers and he will provide them.

GOD USES OTHERS. You may not know how to handle your situation, but there is somebody out there who does. Find that someone. Whenever I (Henry) am dealing with a difficult financial situation, I call a certain friend who has great wisdom in that area, and I lean on him for good advice. I have other people I call for other needs.

After the devastation of divorce, you are wise to seek out people who have knowledge, expertise, and experience in that area—people who have been there, done that, and gotten through it. Keep asking around until you find them.

SEEK STRUCTURED WISDOM. Often recovering from divorce requires more than good advice from friends or others. You may also need structured and professional sources of wisdom. And there are a great number of services out there, including trained counselors, support groups, and psychiatrists. You don't need to reinvent the wheel for your situation. There is help available, already in place.

Don't use cost as an excuse not to take advantage of professional help. Yes, some treatments are expensive, but many are free, and financial assistance is often available from the government and other agencies. Ferret out all your possibilities.

Here is a sampling of places to start looking:

- Professionals in your area of need

- Self-help groups

- Pastors

- Churches

- Community colleges

- Seminars

- Books, tapes, and videos

- Workshops

- Retreats

One caution: Make sure the resources you uncover are authentic. Get referrals from people you trust—your friends, your support group, your doctor, or your pastor.

THE ORDER OF THINGS. God has put you in a universe of order. Things work because of the laws God set in place at creation. Part of the way for you to recover from divorce has already been made in how he created life to work. Your task is to find the wisdom that is already there. So search for his wisdom with all your strength and apply it wholeheartedly.

Leave Your Baggage Behind

We all hate dragging a million pieces of luggage through a crowded airport. What if you had to tote a couple of suitcases, backpacks, and carry-on bags everywhere you went? It would weigh you down and hold you back.

It's the same when recovering from divorce. Emotional baggage can weigh you down and hold you back. Our fourth principle for finding God's way to divorce recovery is to *leave your baggage behind.*

By baggage we mean bad stuff from the past. We've all experienced difficult events and relationships, emotional hurts, serious mistakes, tragic accidents, or loss of a loved one. Ideally, these events are resolved as they happen. But often pain is stuffed instead of dealt with; offenders are not forgiven; fears are not confronted; conflicts are not resolved, leaving us with past feelings and patterns of behavior that impact the present. That's baggage. You can be sure that some of your baggage is directly related to the feelings you face after divorce, and you can't be fully healed until you deal with it.

Here are five practical tips for helping you discard baggage.

1. AGREE THAT YOU HAVE A PAINFUL PAST. Acknowledge that a terribly painful thing has happened to you, involving issues that were not resolved. If you don't work through them, they will prevent your healing. So the first step is to confess to yourself and to God that you have these issues.

2. INCLUDE OTHERS IN YOUR HEALING AND GRIEVING. Seek from others the care and healing you need to resolve these issues. Pouring out your hurt to others who love you opens the door to comfort, encouragement, healing, and support.

3. RECEIVE FORGIVENESS. Getting rid of baggage means being free of the guilt and shame of past failures and sins. God will forgive you for anything you have ever done, no matter how bad. The Bible promises, "For as high as the heavens are above the earth, so great is his love for those who fear him; as far as the east is from the west, so far has he removed our transgressions from us" (Psalm 103:11–12).

Your past failures and mistakes may also have alienated you from certain people. You must go to them, humbly confess your wrong, and receive forgiveness. Once you know you are forgiven, accepted, and loved, you can then re-enter life and begin moving on.

4. FORGIVE OTHERS. Some of your baggage may be hurts you received from others, perhaps your former spouse. You still carry pain, anger, and perhaps hatred. You must forgive these people. Take your cue from God, who has forgiven you. If you don't forgive, resentment will eat away at your heart. When you forgive another, you release that person from your right to exact punishment and retribution from them. As well, you release your own baggage of pain and resentment in the process.

5. SEE YOURSELF THROUGH NEW EYES. Another kind of baggage is the distorted view of ourselves we learned in past relationships or situations. We tend to see ourselves through the eyes of others who are important to us. And depending on whether that view is positive or negative, we either feel valued or devalued. A realistic self-view will be balanced, recognizing strengths as well as weaknesses and growth areas.

Find this view by seeing yourself through God's eyes, for he loves you unconditionally and values you highly. Add to this the view you get from those who love you as God does. Let this *new you* replace the distorted picture that has caused you such grief.

Holding on to the baggage of the past will disable your search for recovery from divorce. Ask God to help you leave it behind.

In your life,

the buck stops with you.

When addressing any problem,

you need to step up

to the plate and take charge.

Own Your Faults and Weaknesses

I n your life, the buck stops with you. When addressing the problems that arise in the aftermath of divorce, you need to step up to the plate and take charge. It's your job to do what God gives you to do. And it's your job to accept the blame for the failures that are truly your own failures, not someone else's. Our fifth principle for God's way to recovery is that you *take responsibility for your life, own up to your faults, and accept blame where it is justified.*

The apostle Paul wrote, "Continue to work out your salvation with fear and trembling, for it is God who works in you to will and to act according to his good purpose" (Philippians 2:12–13). Now that God has saved you, it's your responsibility to live a life that reflects him. But notice that you are not alone in your efforts. God is there with you, empowering you. And this partnership between you and him accomplishes your goal.

Sometimes we have to take responsibility for situations that are not our fault. The man who is unfairly laid off must own up to the situation and start looking for another job. The abused wife must seek counseling.

Determining who is at fault isn't as important as determining who will do something about it. The latter "who" is you. Whoever is at fault, what matters is taking ownership to correct the problem. As you do, God will show you his way.

When we take ownership for what happens in our lives, we are empowered to make changes—to develop plans, tackle situations, and right wrongs. People who take charge of their lives are active people with real initiative. Ownership also frees us from false hopes, from discouragement and passivity, and to take risks and test-drive possible solutions.

When you take ownership and invite God to move in, he does it. He will get involved in moving you to success in overcoming the effects of your divorce. Our role is to seek him, take charge of our own circumstances, and trust him to do for us what only he can do.

Welcome your problems as

gifts from God

to help you

become a better person.

Embrace Problems as Gifts

Some people hit a problem and stop dead in their tracks—they feel stuck and hopeless. All they want is to get rid of it as soon as possible. Other people find something useful in problems. They ask, "What can I learn from this experience? What does God want to change in me?" This is our sixth principle for finding God's way to divorce recovery: *Welcome your problems as gifts from God to help you become a better person.*

There's nothing wrong with trying to solve a problem and alleviate the pain. But instead of rushing to the most immediate fix, we must use the problem to see our lives from God's perspective and find God's way through it.

And God's perspective is quite different. We might compare it to how differently a physician and a patient view pain. You come to the doctor in agony wanting a shot or a pill to make the pain go away. And you want it *now.* But your physician knows your pain is a sign of a deeper problem. He prescribes even more pain: surgery and physical therapy.

It's a choice all of us have to make at some point: You can demand immediate relief, knowing that your problem will recur. Or you can go through the healing process and resolve the problem once and for all. That's the choice you face when dealing with the pain of divorce. God loves you, and like your physician, he is less concerned about your immediate comfort than about your long-term health.

The Bible tells us, "Consider it pure joy, my brothers, whenever you face trials of many kinds, because you know that the testing of your faith develops perseverance" (James 1:2–3). God's way is not *out* of your problem but *through* it. That's how we learn from our difficulties and find God's way.

As you experience the pain that comes from divorce, you first need to look upward, toward God. He is like a storm raining down on a stagnant stream clogged with debris. As the torrent floods the stream, the debris is broken up and the flow resumes.

Second, you must look *inward*. Let God take you on a journey into yourself. He will shine a lantern of truth into the recesses of your heart, illuminating attitudes, wounds, hurts, weaknesses, and perspectives where you need to submit to his touch.

Problems are also a gift in that they help us *normalize* pain—to expect it as a regular part of life.

We tend to think that bad things shouldn't happen to us, and we react in anger, denial, or despair when they do. But this doesn't alter the reality of the pain.

You must give up your protest about the unfairness of your problem and come to a place of acceptance. Only then can you learn what choices, paths, lessons, and opportunities are available to you. Accept pain as part of life. Accept that you don't have all the answers. Acceptance helps us to adapt to the way things really are, and to trust God.

Our problems help us identify with Jesus's sufferings. He loves us deeply, and our rebellion hurts him. But instead of finding a way out, he works through it. While he redeems, restores, and forgives us, he suffers. But he endures it because it's the only way. That is our model for dealing with pain. Identifying with his pain draws us closer to him, to see life as it really is, and patiently take whatever steps are necessary to resolve the problem. Following the pattern of Jesus deepens and matures us.

You should not just passively accept the pain caused by your divorce as the way things will always be, but neither should you ask God to just make the symptoms vanish instantly. Work through it God's way, and accept the gift of what you learn from the process.

We must allow

time for

God to work.

Take Life as It Comes

I (John) have a bone disease called osteopenia. My bones are too porous, and they break easier than normal bones. I am on a special diet and a regimen of bone-strengthening exercises. I get an annual x-ray to check my progress. I would love to get more frequent progress reports, but bones change too slowly for that. The waiting is difficult, but it has taught me that I am not the master of time. I can't speed it up. I must let time have its way.

Our seventh principle for following God's way when we don't know what to do relates to what I am learning through my osteopenia: *We must allow time for God to work.* Though I believe that God performs instantaneous miracles, it seems that his norm is a time-consuming process. Therefore, you must allow time for his process to happen.

Still, it's not easy to wait. When things don't happen quickly, we tend to become impatient, frustrated, and ready to give up. However, those who insist on shortcuts and quick fixes tend to repeat the same problems over and over, getting nowhere.

You've heard the saying "Time heals all wounds." Time heals nothing in and of itself. It's futile to wait passively for God to change circumstances, for help to appear, or for your feelings to change. Such inaction will stick you in a holding pattern where you'll become discouraged when healing doesn't occur. You don't simply wait for a sprained knee to heal. You get a brace and do the physical therapy. Time is the context for our involvement in the process. When you invite God into your life and participate with him in the process, you will begin to see results. So do your part. Seek help and surround yourself with support and accountability. The more engaged you are, the less you will feel the pressure of time.

As nature has seasons, so do our lives. Solomon wrote, "There is a time for everything, and a season for every activity under heaven" (Ecclesiastes 3:1). We can better understand God's timing when we understand the seasons of our lives and identify which we are in.

WINTER. Cold weather and hard ground make things appear dead and unfruitful, but winter can be a very productive time. It's a time to clear out the deadwood, debris, and stones that will hinder future growth; to mend fences and repair broken machinery; to plan and prepare for the growing seasons.

Arrange your schedule and set goals. Research the resources you need, such as a support team, organizations and programs, and counselors. Use winter to prepare.

SPRING. It's a time of new beginnings and fresh hope. You plow the soil, add fertilizer and supplements, plant seeds, and irrigate. You care for the fragile shoots that appear, keeping the garden free of destructive pests.

In the spring of your life, you implement the plans you made in the winter. See a counselor, enter a program, or join a group.

SUMMER. In summer the fields are lush with healthy plants. It's a season for maintenance and protection of what you began in the spring. Don't be lulled into inactivity because good things are happening. Stay with the program; keep working at what God has given you to do.

FALL. At harvesttime you reap what you have sown. You experience and enjoy the benefits of your work.

In the fall of personal growth, you see victory in your battle over the effects of divorce. It's a time of celebration and gratitude. It's a time to give back to God and others something of what you have received.

We would all rather skip the work of winter, spring, and summer and enjoy the harvest of fall all the time. But the only way to reap a bountiful harvest is to make good use of your time in each season.

Getting to

know God and

loving him

with everything you are

is a lifelong journey.

Love God with All You Are

God loves you unconditionally and has a way for you to recover your life and happiness after divorce, even if you can't see it. Following his way is a matter of love on your part. Our eighth principle for following God's way is to *love him passionately with every area of your life.*

Jesus said, "Love the Lord your God with all your heart and with all your soul and with all your mind. This is the first and greatest commandment" (Matthew 22:37–38). Loving God is the greatest commandment because it encompasses all the others.

If we love God, connect to him, and do what honors him, we will find that we are also doing what is best for us. Immerse yourself in his love, and you will find his way to victory.

Here are a few facets of your life where love for God must take the lead.

VALUES. Our values determine what is important to us. Loving God means what is important to him should be important to you.

PASSIONS. These deep urges and drives make us feel alive. Let your love for God fuel your passions.

EMOTIONS. No matter how you feel in your situation—afraid, anxious, sad, or angry—ask God to reach inside you with his love so that you will be able to feel your feelings in ways that help you grow and move on.

TALENTS. Love God with all your strengths, skills, and abilities. As you do, God will use you to make a way for others.

Think of the dearest, closest, most loving relationship you have ever had in your life—even if it's the relationship with your ex in its better days. What characterized this relationship? You were probably very open and vulnerable with each other. You knew each other's secrets, fears, and desires. You took risks with each other. You needed and depended on each other. And this relationship made you feel alive.

Our best human relationships are only a frail picture of the loving, intimate relationship you can enjoy with God. Learning to love him with everything you are is a lifelong journey. And the more of yourself you open up to him, the more God is able to help you through the bad times following your divorce.

Loving God is saying to him, "I don't know what's best for my situation, so I want you to do whatever you need to do in my life." This gives him access to every part of you that needs his love, grace, and support.

You must bring
your problem to
God in order to
experience his love
and healing.

You may feel connected to God in your head, theologically, but not your heart, emotionally. Or the converse may be true. Either way, begin to bring those aspects of your soul and life to his grace so that all of you is being loved and supported by God himself.

If you ever need God's way in your life, it's when you are buried in the debris after the collapse of a marriage and can't find your way out. God has the will and the resources to put your life back together again. "He heals the brokenhearted and binds up their wounds" (Psalm 147:3). However, you must bring your problem to God in order to experience his love and healing.

God is all about love, and he wants us to be all about love too. The more you make everything you are accessible to him, the more you can grow, be healed, and find his way. Be sure you are not hiding the pain of your divorce from God. Love God with your heart, soul, mind, and strength, and let his love set you free. He will show you the way that you can't presently see.

PART II:
DIVORCE AND LOST LOVE

I f you are reading this book because you have experienced divorce or the loss of a love, our heart goes out to you. This experience can be unbelievably brutal.

Randy, a pastor friend of mine (John's), began having marital struggles with Marcie, his wife. At first they seemed like the kind of problems that lots of couples have during the five- to ten-year period of marriage: disconnection, lack of communication, and so on. Then it got worse. Over time it became clear that Marcie didn't want to resolve the issues; she just wanted out. She told Randy that one of them had to move out. She wanted no part of the marriage.

Randy was by no means a perfect guy, but he loved Marcie. He was faithful to her, and he was willing to change anything he could to keep the relationship. He would call me, and we would talk about his options. He diligently did everything he could to put things back together. He asked Marcie to tell him all the ways she was unhappy with him. He listened to her complaints about him without defensiveness. He took ownership of his failings and worked hard to make real and deep changes. He submitted himself to God, the process of growth, and the safe people in his life. He even offered to leave the ministry if that would bring her back.

But it was all to no avail. Marcie left and filed for divorce, and the marriage ended. Randy was devastated. His world, his hopes, and his dreams had all been turned upside down. He still loved and missed Marcie, and yet the marriage was truly over.

This ordeal was difficult enough for Randy, yet something else made matters even worse. Several of his friends had been building up Randy's hopes by assuring him that Marcie would return. They would tell him, "Just trust God and obey, and Marcie will turn around." "Humble yourself, and her eyes will be opened to your love." "God hates divorce, and he will fix this." When Randy felt discouraged by his situation, his friends' assurances would lift his spirits. Then things would get worse, Randy would get down, and his friends would assure him again.

These friends meant well, but the final reality was very different from their assurances. Marcie never came back. She began a new life elsewhere. Sadly, the fact that Randy was not prepared for this possibility hampered his recovery from the loss. God has, since that time, done a lot of healing in Randy; he, too, has a new life and is doing well. At the same time, the false hope unwittingly planted by his friends kept him from believing that Marcie might leave; therefore, when she did go, the shock was worse for him.

Randy's experience points out several realities that anyone who is touched by divorce will come across at some point or another: *Divorce is not a* good thing. Divorce is a real thing. And most of us do not know what to do with it. We are not ready for it. We want to think God will prevent it. We want to believe that something can be done to turn things around.

There is a little of Randy's friends in all of us. At some level, we all protest against the reality of divorce, as it takes so much from us. Yet it is a reality. It is fact. And if you have been through a divorce, are now going through it, or have lost the love of someone to whom you were close, you need to know that God makes a way for you out of the depths into which relational loss can plunge you. Let's explore how you can find his way.

ASSESSING THE DAMAGE

It is impossible to overstate the damage done by divorce. More than just about any of the other losses a person can experience, it permeates every part of your life. It changes your identity from being part of a couple to being a single person. If you have kids, divorce turns their world upside down. Your friends take sides or get weird. You undergo massive lifestyle and geographical changes. The financial implications can be devastating.

Divorce means you have to learn the rules of life all over again. Gone is the safety of knowing you *belong* to someone who will care about you and always be there. You no longer have the blessing of a soulmate with whom you can walk through the joys and tears of life, each feeling what the other feels. Divorce rips away your hopes and dreams of building and growing in love and intimacy. The deepest parts of your soul, where reside the most precious, fragile, and vulnerable parts of your heart, are shattered and torn apart. Divorce breaks your heart. No wonder God thunders that he hates divorce (Malachi 2:16). It breaks the lives and hearts of those he loves.

What is it about divorce that makes it so hard to accept? People can change jobs, roommates, and homes and feel fine. Not so with divorce. It wreaks terrible havoc. We believe the answer to this question is found in the depth and importance of the marriage covenant. If marriage were not so profound, divorce would not be so devastating.

When God created Adam, he designed him for relationship. Every part of Adam was to be emotionally and intimately connected to someone outside himself. God created Adam with a need that only God could fill. Yet God also created within Adam a similar, but different, horizontal need for connectedness. That need was so great that God said it was not good that Adam was alone (that is, in the human-to-human sense; Genesis 2:18). So God created Eve, and she and Adam met that need for each other in the marriage bond. They were one flesh and designed to experience life together, being intimate, caring for each other, and sharing the wonders of the world God had given them to care for. They were two separate people, with their own personalities and thoughts, kept together by oneness of spirit.

Of course, marriage is not the only way that people can meet that deep relational need. Single people can find fulfilling, abiding, deep connectedness in the right sorts of people also. Yet, more than any other type of relationship designed by God, marriage reflects the way that God wants to relate to us. That is why he refers to his people as his bride, in metaphors that instruct us about his love (Isaiah 54:6; Ephesians 5:25–33). Marriage was designed to knit lives and hearts together for life, deepening and strengthening the connection over the years.

So it makes sense that when a marriage is severed, much more about us becomes disconnected than just the relationship with our spouse. On one day, God made two to become one. On another day, the one became two again. Two people who

> The depth that you have loved another is the depth to which that person can hurt you.

were meant to be tightly bonded together became separated, torn asunder from each other. That is why in many wedding sermons you hear Jesus' warning: "So they are no longer two, but one. Therefore what God has joined together, let man not separate" (Matthew 19:6). God designed marriage to be complete and lifelong. His intention is to knit two souls together into a relationship so close and intimate that the fibers of their lives, emotions, minds, and dreams are intertwined in an intricate, complex, and beautiful pattern. Divorce tears apart the fabric of two lives that God has sewn together.

If you are not recovering from your divorce as quickly as you would like, it may simply be an indication that you loved deeply. You likely experienced your marriage as God experienced it. You were deeply committed; you cast your lot in life with a partner and gave unreservedly. You gave up individual conveniences and freedoms for the greater good of the covenant, and you gave your life for something larger than the two of you individually. Is it any wonder that it sometimes takes a long time to move on? You would be able to "get over it and put it behind you" quickly only if there had not been that much there in the first place. *The depth that you have loved another is the depth to which that person can hurt you.* It's as simple as that.

God knows the pain of divorce. He can identify with how you feel. He lost his own "wife," Israel. His people's unfaithfulness wounded him. He said, "I have been grieved by their adulterous hearts" (Ezekiel 6:9). The Hebrew word translated "grieved" here also means "to break or shatter." God knows what it is like to have a broken heart. He has truly "been there."

Grief is not only caused by death. All loss of anything valuable involves grief, and the loss of a relationship may be as close to a death as you can get. It "breaks and shatters" us. That kind of hurt doesn't just evaporate immediately; it must submit to a process of grief. And, as we said, the deeper the love, the deeper will be that grief—the breaking and shattering that we must endure and heal.

Some people who understand this principle choose not to love deeply in order to protect themselves from the devastating hurt that the loss of love can bring. But in spite of the potential pain, the rewards of love are so incredibly great as to make it well worth the risk. The only way to be fully human—and fully godlike—is to love. And the more we love, the more fully human and godlike we become. Our example is God himself, who took the risk of loving us and endured terrible pain because of it. Yet he did it because love is the ultimate nature of all goodness. Love is, as the old saying goes, "what makes the world go round." But that doesn't minimize the pain we endure when love fails. It hurts. Badly. And we must find God's way to deal with it.

God is with you—and even though you may not know how to pull yourself out of the devastating aftermath of divorce, be assured that he always makes a way for his own. You are not left to grieve and be stuck in pain forever. Dealing with divorce is not simply a matter of coping with the pain, accepting it, and hanging on in faith until one day you escape your misery by going to heaven. God has something much, much better for you than that. Your divorce may not have been intended or designed by God, but he has a way through this that is good for you.

BECOMING THE PERSON GOD WANTS YOU TO BE

What follows are some of the issues that occur in a life after divorce. Your ability to work through these will be critical to your recovery from the divorce's effects. With God's help you can work through the pain and come out on the other end a better, more mature, and more complete person.

What was once a "we" has now become an "I." In marriage, God brings two people together to form a union for life. The two think of life in terms of a pairing: where *we* want to go on vacation, what *we* want to do about having children, who *our* friends are, and so forth. Marriage means letting go of individual conveniences and interpreting personal desires in terms of the greater good of the marriage. If I am weak, we can be strong together. We bear the load, the responsibilities, and the burdens of life together. We think in terms of "we." "We" shapes our identity, the way we see ourselves in the world, and how we belong.

Divorce ends the "we" and brings you back to "I." You no longer have a soulmate to count on, dream with, and go to for help with life's constant barrage of problems. The divorced person is alone again, but this time it's in a different way than that of a never-married person. It is not simply a matter of resetting the switch to "single" and going on from there as if nothing had happened. The divorced person *has known and experienced* marriage. For many divorced people, losing the "we-ness" and reverting to being an "I" again is almost intolerable. They miss the benefits and experiences of marriage so much that the single life seems insipid and bland. These people find singleness so intolerable, in fact, that they often rebound into a relationship that is not right for them, simply to get out of the pain of their isolation and loneliness.

However, God has a way for you to bring good out of this bad situation.

First, *you can develop and grow into the individual God created you to be.* God meant marriage to be a union of two distinct people with distinct opinions, viewpoints, and values, who each contribute to the growth of the other. As the old saying goes, "If you never disagree, then one of you is not necessary." Ideally, we are to experience our existence both as an individual and as a couple. Yet when one spouse lacks individuality, it can cause major disruptions in the marriage.

Sometimes the reason for divorce is that one mate did not develop his or her own individual soul or have a strong sense of self. The undeveloped spouse may bore or smother the other. Sometimes one spouse will control or dominate the other to the degree that the less dominant one loses a sense of self. Sometimes a spouse will neglect his or her inner growth and development, believing it more important to make a good marriage than to assert one's own individuality, never realizing that a marriage is only as good as the two souls that comprise it.

Does any of this ring true for you? Have you allowed your individuality to become smothered or diminished because you thought it would help the marriage? Divorce can be a wake-up call to own and be aware of the many treasures and talents that God has uniquely given you. If divorce has caused you to realize that you have lost your true self—or never even found it—you can view the new world created by the divorce as an opportunity to grow individually and personally.

This is both good news and bad news. The bad news is that you must now make your own decisions. The good news is that you *can* now make your own decisions. Rather than hiding behind marriage to avoid dealing with choices, freedom, opportunities, and problems, begin to use the time after divorce as a season of finding what you love, hate, are talented in, desire, and have a vision for. Make your new single state a time of exploration and seeking God's ways for your life. As Jesus said, "But seek first his kingdom and his righteousness, and all these things will be given to you as well" (Matthew 6:33).

That's what my friend Ruth did. When she was married, Ruth was like the subordinated "we" person we described earlier. She had no life of her own and was dependent on whatever her husband said or thought. After they divorced, she felt lost on her own, with no significant individuality to make singleness work. Therefore, she went on a search for the person God had wanted her to be all along. She learned all she could; she took courses, got mentoring, and began making forays into the business world. In time, this homemaker mom found that she had a real knack for business and making money. She is now a successful businesswoman, has found that her life is quite meaningful and interesting, and feels that she has a lot to contribute. When she marries again she will have a lot to bring to the relationship, and her husband will be the better for it.

Second, after your divorce *you have the opportunity to discover the richness of life apart from marriage.* Life is more than marriage. God intended us to find a relationship with him, a community of safe people, meaningful tasks, and a mission and purpose in order to have a good life on this earth. Marriage is one of the best experiences this life has to offer. However, marriage is not life; it is part of life. And for many, life does not ever include marriage.

Yet many divorced people tend to conceptualize life in terms of marriage. They feel incomplete and lost without a spouse and look for a new mate far too quickly. This is, at its base, not really a desire for marriage; it is a fear-based reaction to the unknown. If you find yourself in this situation, look at building a life for yourself rather than making marriage an equivalent to life. As they say, "Get a life." Let go of the demand that you need to be married to be complete. This will allow you to find and experience all the other aspects of life that are available in a well-rounded and balanced existence. Many people who have done this have later met someone else who also has a life; then they have built a new marriage together that is far stronger and closer than either one of them had dreamed.

> Grief is accepting the reality of what is.

EMBRACING GRIEF AND LOSS

A divorce is, by definition, a loss. In fact, one of the Hebrew words for divorce speaks of "cutting or severing a bond." Something has been lost. The loss is real and deep, and, as we mentioned briefly already, it must be grieved.

Grief is accepting the reality of what is. It is internalizing the reality of the death of the marriage on both the intellectual and emotional levels. That is grief's job and purpose—to allow us to come to terms with the way things really are so that we can move on. Grief is a gift of God. Without it, we would all be condemned to a life of continually denying reality, arguing or protesting against reality, and never growing from the realities we experience.

When you allow yourself to embrace the sadness and shed the tears for what you have lost through divorce, then you can move on to a new phase of life when grief tells you it is time. It is important to note that *those who have not fully grieved the losses of their divorce are in jeopardy of either never getting over it or repeating it.* When I (John) am speaking to groups of divorced people, I often talk about this in terms of dating. I'll tell them, "When someone you are seeing tells you that his (or her) divorce wasn't that hard on him and he really didn't have a difficult time with it, don't sit there another second. Rush to the door and burn rubber getting out of the driveway." A person who hasn't grieved a significant loss has unfinished business inside. Whatever is lurking there can cause others great harm and grief.

What does it mean to embrace grief in divorce? It means many things, including:

- Allowing painful feelings to come and go, without prohibiting them

- Reaching out to others to comfort and support you through the grieving process, rather than going it alone

- Putting an end to the protests and arguments in your head about how it shouldn't have happened, or whose fault it was or was not

Grief does not allow us to be right, strong, and in control. Grief is starkly simple. Basically it says, "You loved and you lost. It hurts." Yet God is on the other side, waiting, with his safe people, to catch us as we fall, hold tightly to us in love, and restore us to joy.

One of the most difficult yet important tasks of grief in divorce is that of *remembering and experiencing value for the loved one.* Let yourself feel the love you still may bear for your former spouse, the positive emotions, your desires for togetherness, and your appreciation for that person's good traits and characteristics. Most people who are trying to get past divorce don't recognize the importance of this, thinking instead that they need to focus on the other person's faults, sins, and mistakes. Sometimes they do this out of a desire for revenge. At other times it is a reaction against the need they feel for the person, which causes them to fear getting hooked back in. Sometimes they do this as a way to complete the letting-go process.

Yet grief does not work in this way. When you let go of a love, you are to let go of the whole person: good and bad, weaknesses and strengths, positives and negatives. When we allow ourselves to feel only the negative feelings, we then let go only of the person we dislike, which is just a part of the whole individual. We won't grieve the other part—the good part—the person we still love and want, and with whom we have in our memories a repository of good experiences. Therefore that person remains in our present world, still active within our heart and causing all sorts of difficulties.

Let go of the desire to see only the bad, and allow yourself to appreciate and let go of the good person you are leaving. This is the key to freedom beyond grief in divorce.

TAKING STOCK OF YOUR CONTRIBUTIONS

When I (John) speak to divorced groups, I often ask, "Now that you are divorced, what is your single biggest problem?" Invariably, someone says, "My ex!" We all laugh, and then I get serious and say, "Well, if anyone here truly believes that, they are pretty much doomed. Because if your biggest problem is not yourself, your soul, and your areas of growth, and if you are more invested in the failings of your ex than in yourself, then your ex still controls your every move."

That statement generally makes for a lively discussion. But it's true. If all you can see are the faults of your former spouse, you are helpless. You have nothing to work on, change, or improve. You have no way to alter the course of your life for the better.

Your ex is gone, and you have no influence over him or her anymore. Your focus on your former spouse's faults is meaningless because it's an exercise that leads you nowhere. That's why one of the most helpful things you can do after a divorce is to take stock of your own contributions to the problems in your marriage—identifying and admitting where you screwed up, where you were unloving, or where you hurt your spouse. If you do this growth exercise, you will gain a lot. You will put yourself in a position to solve whatever internal problems you had, and thus be more objective about any problems the other person has. Jesus said, "First take the plank out of your own eye, and then you will see clearly to remove the speck from your brother's eye" (Matthew 7:5).

This task has nothing to do with making you feel bad or guilty about the past. What is done is done. *It has everything to do with ensuring that you grow beyond the mistakes of the past and do not re-create them in your future.* The huge benefit to this kind of self-assessment is that it will keep you from repeating past mistakes. It will enable you to enter a new relationship with a much better chance of success.

We have never

seen a divorce in

which it was

100 percent one

person's fault.

Though many times one spouse is very much more at fault than the other, we have never seen a divorce in which it was 100 percent one person's fault and 0 percent the other person's. Even the most loving, faithful, and righteous person can contribute to the problems in a marriage. To deny this is to prevent great growth and preservation for the future.

Here is a brief list of problems that partners typically contribute to the destruction of a marriage. Look at these and be willing to own, change, and grow through any that may apply to you—whether you were the "bad guy" in the marriage, the "good guy," or somewhere in between:

WITHDRAWAL OF LOVE. You removed the very glue that the other person needed to feel secure and valued.

CONTROL. You did not allow your spouse to have his or her own feelings, opinions, and decisions separate from yours without some sort of punitive response on your part.

UNLOVING CRITICISM. You put down your spouse out of anger, a sense of superiority, or not being able to accept who he or she is.

IRRESPONSIBILITY. You did not take ownership of your part in making the marriage work.

PASSIVITY. You made the other person take on too much responsibility because you avoided making decisions.

DECEPTION. You were untruthful in love, time, money, or your whereabouts.

MORAL SUPERIORITY. You saw only your ex's faults and your spiritual or moral higher ground. It's a form of arrogance and pride.

CODEPENDENCY. You rescued your spouse, or

enabled him or her to stay irresponsible when you should have let the consequences bring him or her to responsibility.

Ask God to show you what things you may need to change. As you bring these issues before God and your friends, you can then safely work on them and improve yourself. When you do this, you will find that in the future you'll have the discernment and ability to choose better people as potential partners and become a better person yourself.

KNOWING WHEN TO DATE AGAIN

Divorced people often ask, "When can I start dating again?" We carefully avoid the smarty reply, "Whenever you find someone who will say yes when you ask." It is a good question and needs to be answered carefully. While divorced people don't want to make the same mistakes again, they do want to go out and meet the right sorts of people. Though we are convinced that personal and spiritual growth are the real work of the day, and that dating should come second, we do believe that dating is a very good thing.

Here are some things to do and know before you jump into the dating scene after a divorce.

1. WAIT. It is wise to wait until you have stabilized, grieved, and grown through the effects of your divorce. Be sure that you have gone through this necessary process. To begin dating while separated and not divorced, or immediately after a divorce is finalized, is to risk covering up or minimizing what you need to learn, feel, and experience about this major event. Give yourself adequate time for God to help you work through the effects of the divorce and rebuild your stability.

2. DEVELOP A LONG-TERM AND STABLE RELATIONSHIP WITH GOD. Work on getting to know him and his ways. Seek him and his life and guidance. He will help you to know when you are

ready to date again. Often, as people develop their spiritual lives, they find fullness in knowing that God takes the edge off any desire to be in the dating world.

3. GET CONNECTED TO A COMMUNITY OF HEALTHY, STABLE, LOVING, AND HONEST PEOPLE. Make them your "family," the place where you bring your life, your needs, and your struggles. People who have supportive communities often find that they are not as desperate to be married, because their community is meeting some of the needs that drive their urge to marry. This frees them to date and marry according to their values, their freedom, and their choice, rather than their fears and needs. It keeps them off a timetable and prevents desperation. You will find great benefits in being deeply emotionally invested in non-dating relationships, which in turn will help healthy dating relationships spring forth.

If you are divorced or have lost a love, you may be thinking of yourself as damaged goods. This is not at all how God sees you. He knows all our frailties and empathizes with them. He does not want to condemn. He desires more than anything to restore and redeem his people to himself.

You may be damaged, but God can repair the damage. No damage is beyond his repair. You may feel that you are now of second-class status, but God is the God of fresh starts and renewal. Go to him with your past and your present, and ask him to show you the way to a life of renewal: "And the God of all grace, who called you to his eternal glory in Christ, after you have suffered a little while, will himself restore you and make you strong, firm and steadfast" (1 Peter 5:10).

PART III:
BEGIN YOUR JOURNEY TODAY

Y ou are near the end of this book, but you are only at the beginning of the journey God is making for you to recover fully from your divorce. You may have come to this book not knowing what to do in the face of your pain. We have shown you that God has a way for you, and we have tried to prepare you to walk in that way. In the earlier sections we filled your pack with supplies and put a map in your hands. Now it's time for you to hit the trail. As you do, we leave you with three final words of advice.

WALK IN GRACE. Your first step on the journey, and every subsequent step, is a step into God's grace. Simply put, grace is God's *unmerited favor*. This means that God is on your side. He wants to heal the wounds of your divorce and is committed to work in you, with you, and through you to accomplish it. God loves you completely, and he's going with you every step of the way. He will be your biggest cheerleader.

STEP OUT IN FAITH. You need two strong legs to complete a strenuous hike—right, left, right, left, one after the other. Similarly, in your journey with God, faith is a two-step process. It is both an *attitude* and an *action*. You believe God loves you, but you need to love him in return. You know God will speak to you, but you need to listen attentively. You have faith that God will guide you and protect you, but you need to follow him and submit to his care. Whenever you take a step of *faith* in God, follow it with a step of *action*.

STAY ON THE TRAIL. Now that your feet are moving, let's take one last look at the trail ahead. This is the way God has made for you. It may be strenuous in trying times, but it is full of discovery and wonder. And the destination is well worth the effort. Here are ten key reminders that will help keep you on the trail and moving forward.

1. Set goals. What do you want God to do for you? Decide now, and be specific. Make your goal as clear and concise as possible so you can envision it, pray about it, and decide on a specific strategy to reach it.

2. Record progress. Write down your goal and put it where you can see it often—on the fridge, on the bathroom mirror, in your daily planner or journal, beside your desk or workstation, etc. Also, write down each significant insight as you step toward your goal.

3. Gather resources. Start looking for the people, programs, and organizations who can assist you on the journey. The better your resources, the faster you should reach your goal.

4. Acquire information. Educate yourself on the kinds of problems that divorced people face. Studies show that those who are more knowledgeable about their condition do better in the treatment of it. They ask insightful questions and sometimes notice things about their condition, feelings, or solutions they might otherwise miss. As much as possible, become an expert in all aspects of post-divorce problems and recovery.

5. Identify tasks. Give yourself specific assignments: thought patterns to adopt, actions to perform, emotions to express, habits to form, and so forth. Break your tasks into manageable portions and take them one by one.

6. Evaluate progress. Review your progress toward recovery at defined intervals. Are you making headway? If not, why not? Put your evaluation in writing for future reference, and make any necessary adjustments to your plan.

7. **Explore preferences.** Tailor your plan and tasks to your individual preferences. You will likely have many choices on your journey: counselors, programs, classes, and organizations.

8. **Remain flexible.** Don't cast your plan in stone. It exists to serve your recovery and growth. If your plan is not getting results over a reasonable period of time, rethink it and make changes. And even when your plan is working, stay alert to ways you can improve it.

9. **Pray continually.** When you pray, you're not talking to the wall or to yourself. You are talking to God, and he hears you and responds. Prayer is a genuine and powerful ally on your journey. It's not your prayers that have the power; it's God on the other end of the line who has the power to do what you cannot do. Don't take one step without talking to God about it.

10. **Pace yourself.** This is a journey, not a race. Few changes happen overnight, no matter

how hard you work or pray. Give God time to work, and be thankful for the little changes you see.

We are pleased that you are so interested in following God's way to recovery from divorce. We pray that the God in whom we live, move, and exist will guide and sustain you on the journey, both today and forever. God bless you!

—Henry Cloud, Ph.D.
—John Townsend, Ph.D.
Los Angeles, California

Prayer is

a genuine and

powerful ally

on your journey.

EMBARK ON A
LIFE-CHANGING JOURNEY
OF PERSONAL AND SPIRITUAL GROWTH

DR. HENRY CLOUD   **DR. JOHN TOWNSEND**

Dr. Henry Cloud and Dr. John Townsend have been bringing hope and healing to millions for over two decades. They have helped people everywhere discover solutions to life's most difficult personal and relational challenges. Their material provides solid, practical answers and offers guidance in the areas of *parenting, singles issues, personal growth,* and *leadership.*

Bring either Dr. Cloud or Dr. Townsend to your church or organization. They are available for:

- Seminars on a wide variety of topics
- Training for small group leaders
- Conferences
- Educational events
- Consulting with your organization

Other opportunities to experience Dr. Cloud and Dr. Townsend:

- Ultimate Leadership workshops—held in Southern California throughout the year
- Small group curriculum
- Seminars via Satellite
- Solutions Audio Club—Solutions is a weekly recorded presentation

For other resources, and for dates of seminars and workshops
by Dr. Cloud and Dr. Townsend, visit:
www.cloudtownsend.com

For other information **Call (800) 676-HOPE (4673)**

Or write to:
Cloud-Townsend Resources
3176 Pullman Street, Suite 105
Costa Mesa, CA